Imagine!

Marc Maurer
Editor

Large Type Edition

A KERNEL BOOK
published by
NATIONAL FEDERATION OF THE BLIND

TABLE OF CONTENTS

EDITOR'S INTRODUCTION

Five years ago we in the National Federation of the Blind set for ourselves the task of building a research and training institute on blindness. It was to be a place where our hopes and dreams for the future could be shaped and molded and brought to concrete reality through the work such an institute could accomplish.

This year we opened the Institute. The Governor of the State of Maryland, the senior United States Senator from the State of Maryland, and the Mayor of the City of Baltimore were all in attendance at the Grand Opening, where we named our new building and the programs it will create the National Federation of the Blind Jernigan Institute in honor of the longtime leader and builder of our movement, the late Dr. Kenneth Jernigan.

The Institute is, indeed, a monument to the imaginative spirit and dynamic leadership of Dr. Jernigan. But it is far more than that. It is the visible embodiment of the creative energy that lives within the heart of the organization itself.

Through this energy and with the Jernigan Institute to focus and direct it, we will *Imagine* the future we want for ourselves into being:

Imagine that future where a handheld pocket reading machine will enable a blind person to read with ease print of any kind on any object which is encountered!

Imagine that future where nonvisual tactile and audio techniques for accessing data permit talented blind children to excel in science education!

Imagine that future where blind seniors continue on with their active lifestyles because of innovative new training methods!

Marc Maurer, President
National Federation of the Blind

Imagine that future where the ordinary classroom teacher can teach Braille effectively to any blind student!

And most of all *Imagine* that future, where those of us who are blind are living and working side by side with our sighted neighbors and friends, and neither we nor they give hardly a second thought to our blindness because all of the misunderstandings and misconceptions as well as the information access barriers have been overcome.

This is where all of you who have come to be a real part of our movement through the pages of these Kernel Books are essential. Our energy alone cannot jump the gap between where we are now and where we must go in order for that future to become a reality.

Your creative energy must be joined to that of the individuals you will meet in the pages of this twenty-seventh Kernel Book:

the blind man who loves to tour antique auto shows; the blind woman with her "mirror, mirror on the wall"; the blind student turned away from a haunted house at an amusement park; and yes, even the blind teenage Easter bunny.

We look forward to what lies ahead with anticipation and excitement. What is good for us will be good also for those in the broader society. Together with the promise of the Jernigan Institute and the energies of our sighted brothers and sisters joined to our own, we will *Imagine* into existence a future that is bright with hope and filled with joy.

Marc Maurer
Baltimore, Maryland
2004

WHY LARGE TYPE?

The type size used in this book is 14-point for two important reasons: One, because typesetting of 14-point or larger complies with federal standards for the printing of materials for visually impaired readers, and we want to show you what type size is helpful for people with limited sight.

The second reason is that many of our friends and supporters have asked us to print our paperback books in 14-point type so they too can easily read them. Many people with limited sight do not use Braille. We hope that by printing this book in a larger type than customary, many more people will be able to benefit from it.

The Institute, the Queen, and the Reading Machine

by Marc Maurer

Some people believe that history is a set of accidental occurrences that come together without plan or pattern. In my work as President of the National Federation of the Blind I have occasionally made arguments that support this theory. For example, when I am teaching leadership classes I sometimes tell people that the reason we in the United States speak English instead of French is that one woman in Europe called another woman sister.

The story goes this way. In 1534 the French explorer Jacques Cartier discovered the St. Lawrence River and claimed the land surrounding it for France. In 1607 English settlers landed at Jamestown, Virginia, and in 1620 other English settlers landed at Plymouth, Massachusetts. The land surrounding these settlements and the territory between were claimed for England.

In 1682 another French explorer, La Salle, traveled down the Mississippi River to the Gulf of Mexico and claimed all of the land drained by the river for King Louis XIV. The northern and central sections of the North American continent were French territory. Most of the eastern seaboard belonged to the British Empire.

In 1756 a war began between France and England. In Europe it became known as the Seven Years War, and in North America it is now called the French and Indian War. In North America the final battle occurred on the Plains of Abraham outside of Quebec. The French army was led by the Marquis de Montcalm and the British by General James Wolfe. Both generals had requested reinforcements for the battle, but General Montcalm did not get them.

In the French court a woman known as Madame de Pompadour had become a favorite of the king. Maria Theresa was the empress of the Austro-Hungarian Empire. Maria Theresa had written to Madame de Pompadour addressing her as sister, which is the designation one queen used when writing to another. Madame de Pompadour was not the queen, and she had not been well received at the French court. She was flattered by being addressed in such a queenly fashion.

When Maria Theresa was faced with an invasion of the empire, she asked for French troops to help. The king sent his soldiers east instead of west, and Montcalm, who historians say was the better general, was defeated by Wolfe, and Canada became British territory.

With the defeat of the French army, the influence of France in North America diminished, and the language of the country that would become the United States was established as English.

Part of my responsibility as President of the National Federation of the Blind is to explain why we face the circumstances that exist. Much planning has been done about blindness and the blind, but a great deal of it focuses on separating blind people from the rest of society.

In the past almshouses for the blind have been created, and sheltered workshops have been established where the blind were assigned to do simple, repetitive, undemanding tasks. However, what we want is not to be separated from society but to be welcomed within it.

In 1999 we talked about building an institute where we could dream of a brighter tomorrow for the blind and conduct the necessary research to make the dream a reality. For the past five years we have been planning, collecting our resources, examining construction documents, negotiating contracts, and searching for the talent that we need to operate the institute. We have named the building after our great president, Dr. Kenneth Jernigan. The National Federation of the Blind Jernigan Institute is a monument to the imaginative spirit and dynamic leadership of Dr. Jernigan, and we have already begun to stimulate the development of new products and new services for the blind.

In the mid-1970's we met a bright young engineer, Dr. Raymond Kurzweil, who was just coming from MIT. Dr. Kurzweil wanted to know what blind people needed, and we told him that a reading machine could help to give us access to information. He invented the first reading machine for the blind.

It was so impressive that Walter Cronkite, the television commentator and news broadcaster, ended the news broadcast on January 13, 1976, by having the reading machine sign off with his signature phrase, "And that's the way it was, January 13, 1976."

At the groundbreaking for the Jernigan Institute in October of 2001, I speculated that with the proper effort we could build a reading machine small enough to fit into a briefcase or a pocket—the handheld reading machine. Today, we are building the Kurzweil-National Federation of the Blind Reader. The first prototype is already available. It consists of a tablet PC (a computer smaller than a laptop) connected to a handheld digital camera.

This device can be used to "read" printed information. It captures the image of print and makes it audible, and it can "read" documents, computer screens, digital readouts on LCD displays, and other information. We will be testing the reading machine for several months, and we expect to make it available to blind people within the next year.

Most of the time blind people recognize others through sound. The timber of a voice, speech patterns, the pattern of shoe heels—these are details that indicate the identity of the individual. Some sighted people like to play a game with the blind. They like to come up and say, "Tell me who I am." Sometimes they try to make the game more interesting for them by disguising their voices. This is dull for the blind.

Imagine what a reading machine with powerful processing technology and substantial memory could do. The pictures of members of the legislature could be loaded into the memory of the reading machine. The machine could capture the image of a person in the crowd and compare it to the library of information available. The blind person would then be informed of the identity of the human beings at a meeting or gathering.

The reading machine might also incorporate images such as chairs, desks, and other furniture. It might be able to direct a blind person in a crowded theatre to an empty seat. With enough computer power, it might be able to describe the action on the screen after the blind person has taken that chair.

When this device becomes available, it will be light enough and powerful enough to read documents at a conference or in class, and it can be used to gain information from public information kiosks or from the digital display on the microwave. It should provide many, many new opportunities for the blind.

For the blind, history has largely been a collection of random events that occurred mostly by happenstance. However, with the coming of the National Federation of the

Blind, the blind have been able to take a hand in creating our own history. For the first time blind people have found the means to determine what the future will be, and we have asked our sighted friends and neighbors to join with us in making it as bright as possible. Sometimes we will create technology to give us information or to help us in other ways. Sometimes we will dream of training classes that offer new perspective or educational opportunities. Sometimes we will seek the understanding and support of our sighted neighbors and colleagues to help us bring to those who have lost their sight a measure of hope.

No matter what the program may be, we will do what we can to anticipate the future and to plan to implement programs that are good for us and for others in the community. We have been able to dream so much and to build so well because of the assistance you have offered. Tomorrow is the history we have planned to write—we look forward to it with joy.

ON THE ROAD AGAIN

by Larry Streeter

Larry Streeter is president of the National Federation of the Blind of Idaho. He lives in Boise with his wife Sandy. They are active in their community and pursue their mutual interests with vigor. Here Larry describes an unusually satisfactory Saturday morning outing. Here is what he has to say:

I have always had a great interest in antique cars, and so when the opportunity came to attend a weekend function to view a wide variety of unique autos, I boarded the bus with my wife Sandy and off we went. The show was being held at the Boise train depot, which is no longer used for passenger service.

Larry Streeter

As we trudged up the hill to see the cars, I became rather excited. This was my first antique car show in years; the last opportunity had occurred many years before in Canton, Ohio. I was around 20 years old then and fondly remembered the event.

There were more than forty cars at the depot that brisk Saturday morning: several Model T and Model A Fords, and a 1916 Studebaker Touring Car, which the owner described as the early 7-passenger family mini van. We also noted a 1923 Ford Pickup, a 1931 Plymouth, an Oldsmobile or two, and a 1935 Bentley to name just a few. To tell the truth, I couldn't keep track of them all, but the colors were as wide a variety as the makes and models we viewed.

As we moved from car to car, we would pose questions to the owners, who were very friendly and most willing and available to respond to each and every question. At first, we did not touch the vehicles, but after a short while, we were encouraged by several owners to take a closer look.

After nearly an hour going from one car to another, one couple, Mr. and Mrs. Street by name, started talking to us. We asked a few questions about their car, a 1931 red and black Model A Coupe. Then suddenly, Mrs. Street asked where we lived. I told her our address, and in return inquired as to where she lived. She responded with a street address that I recognized. She made a statement to her husband about coming by our house, picking us up, and taking us for a ride. Mr. Street said that would be great, but then looked her way again and stated something like, "Why don't we take them right now." He followed up by stating that he could take Sandy first and then come back and get me. To say the least, we were both elated.

Sandy moved toward the door opposite the driver and got in. Mr. Street looked at me and stated he would be back shortly. As many may know, a Model A often comes with a rumble seat. A rumble seat or "Dickey" as it was sometimes called, is an extra external seat that could be accessed by lifting a forward opening trunk lid in the rear of the car. I asked Mr. Street if I could ride in the rumble seat. He promptly stated that if I could get in, then that would work just fine.

He immediately explained how to get into the seat by stepping on certain areas of the back fender. He told me not to worry about putting my feet on the seat but said that you kind of "have to dive in feet first." This I did with a great deal of gusto. It was a most comfortable leather seat.

He started the Model A, and off we went for about a fifteen-minute ride. Our speed never exceeded twenty-five miles an hour even though we were told it would kick up to forty-five. As we drove through several neighborhoods, I definitely felt the cool breeze blowing; it seemed like it was coming from every direction. Mr. Street told Sandy that he was concerned that I might be a little cold riding in the rumble seat, but she assured him that it would not matter to me for I was truly in my own little world at that moment in time. Yes, Mr. Street was on target; it was quite chilly, but I would have nearly frozen to death for that wonderful experience.

We returned to the depot. Sandy was far more knowledgeable about this particular 1931 Model A. Upon our arrival, I climbed out of the rumble seat. We expressed our appreciation more than once to Mr. and Mrs. Street. I told them it was the thrill of my life. Never in my wildest dreams did I think that such a unique experience could happen.

My attitudes about blindness come from a strong father and mother who insisted that I could compete on terms of equality with my sighted friends and neighbors and that it was extremely important to be involved in the community. When I joined the National Federation of the Blind over twenty-eight years ago, I already had a positive attitude about blindness: who I, as a blind person, was and what I could do if I used the talents that had been given to me. The National Federation of the Blind without a doubt has certainly helped further to mold my character. Throughout the years, I have always tried to be involved in a variety of activities—sports, church, work, and travel just to mention a few.

The NFB is more than an organization— it is a way of life. I made a decision long ago to heed those words from my parents that I would never allow my blindness to stop me from participating fully in our society.

We could have stayed at home that recent Saturday morning, learned little or nothing about antique cars, and never met some very interesting people. But we chose to be seen with our fellow sighted citizens. They observed our independent nature, and we learned from them as well. We had a great time and will always recall one fantastic ride in that red and black Model A with its rumble seat.

MIRROR, MIRROR ON THE WALL

by Nancy Burns

Nancy Burns is president of the National Federation of the Blind of California. She enjoys being stylishly dressed. In her story, "Mirror, Mirror on the Wall," Nancy shares some of the simple techniques she has developed for accomplishing this task as a totally blind woman. Here is what she has to say:

Recently, on the way to the National Federation of the Blind of California office, a woman stopped me as I stepped out of the elevator. She said, "May I ask you a question?" This often happens to me, and I'm sure to other blind people, as we move about the world. People are curious about

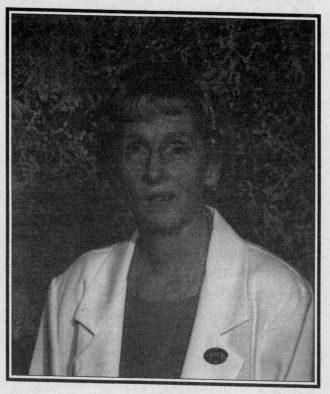

Nancy Burns

this or that, and I always try to answer such questions.

I responded, "Sure." She then said, "You always look so well coordinated; how do you manage your wardrobe?" This is a frequently asked question. I suppose that the majority of the sighted world believes that since I am blind I should not look well coordinated. I have several pat responses to this often-asked question. I said to her that it really wasn't all that difficult and that I had an assignment for her. I suggested that she explore her closet by touch and that she would probably be surprised at how many items of clothing she could identify in this manner. The woman agreed to do this, and hopefully she followed through with her assignment.

My responses to this question vary with the circumstances of the encounter. With this quick meeting in the hallway I knew my response needed to be short and to the point. Under different circumstances I might have spent a little more time explaining the various methods of identifying clothes.

There are probably as many methods of labeling clothes as there are blind people. There is no right or wrong way to do this; there just needs to be a system that works.

Many items are easily identifiable by touch. For those of us who know Braille, there are several options. Braille tags can be sewn or pinned to a particular garment. In the case of blazers or pants, which are very similar in style and material, I simple write the color on a Braille card and put it into the pocket.

Some people like to arrange their clothing by color. For example, black skirts, blouses, or pants can be placed in the closet with a rubber band or string to keep them all together. Other people establish a system of safety pins to identify colors, perhaps one safety pin for black, two for brown, et cetera, pinned inside a waistband of a skirt or pants.

The process of matching colors is an eternal challenge for blind or visually impaired people. Technology has come a long way, but there is no device that will tell me if this shade of red matches the red in my blouse. It is at this point that I suggest that all blind and visually impaired people need a "talking mirror." This mirror comes in the form of a spouse, friend, or relative who has good taste and is willing to be brutally honest. We all need feedback in this area, and it is important to find such a person.

Store clerks are sometimes willing to answer questions, but if you don't know the individual, this may be a gamble. There are times when I have not had my talking mirror with me, and I have resorted to asking other women shoppers. I remember one occasion when I was cruising through a sales rack and found a very nice blazer. My husband, who was with me at the time but who is legally blind and has great difficulty with colors, believed it to be purple. Two women shoppers were looking through the same sales rack. I held the jacket up and said, "Excuse me, but could you please tell me the color of this blazer?" I knew from overhearing their conversation that they were serious shoppers. They were delighted to stop and describe the color of the jacket and even to suggest colors that would match up nicely with it.

I have experienced several of these impromptu meetings in department stores. They generally result in great conversations and help to break the ice with the public about blindness. Most people are willing to help, and the resulting conversations are often fun and sometimes prove to be learning experiences for the sighted person.

A few years ago I met Elaine, who was experiencing recent vision loss. She had worked in an exclusive boutique on Rodeo

Drive. She lamented to me how sad she was that she could no longer coordinate her clothes and complete the outfit with accessories, such as scarves and pins. Her closet was filled with beautiful clothes that she no longer wore. She simply relied upon a few basic outfits.

Elaine had a friend in her apartment building who could help her now and then, but she did not want to bother her too often. I suggested that while her friend was there she could hang a skirt and matching blouse on the same hanger. I further suggested that she could even place a matching scarf or pin on the outfit as it hung in the closet. This was simply a way of rethinking for Elaine. Once she got the hang of it she was delighted and began wearing her beautiful clothes, including scarves and pins that she had packed away after losing her sight.

As far as applying makeup is concerned, this is mainly a matter of practice. Your talking mirror is an important initial part of this process. Once you know what shades and colors work with your skin tones, applying makeup simply becomes a routine matter.

Blind or visually impaired men should also find a person to provide reliable feedback. Matching shirts, ties, jackets, and pants can be handled by any of the above-suggested methods. Shirts and matching ties can be easily placed on the same hanger. Appropriate belts can also be looped over the same hanger.

Spots or stains on clothing can sometimes present a challenge. This, again, is when your talking mirror becomes incredibly valuable and needs to be brutally honest. It is important to have a spouse or friend advise you of a spot so that it may be properly washed or cleaned.

The bottom line to all of this wardrobe mystery is simply to find a working system. For those who have recently lost their sight, it is a matter of rethinking their organizational methods. A person, blind or sighted, who is well dressed generally appears more confident and self-assured than one who pays little attention to his or her wardrobe. Coordinating and maintaining a fashionable wardrobe is no big deal for a blind person; it simply takes a little thought and a desire to do so.

FRIGHT NIGHT

by Monty Anderson

Monty Anderson is a board member of the Honolulu Chapter of the National Federation of the Blind of Hawaii and is a graduate student in the Speech Department at the University of Hawaii at Manoa. He also serves as president of our Student Division in Hawaii. His story offers a thoughtful reflection on the treatment he received when he attempted to visit a Haunted House. Here is what he has to say:

"How ya doing, Bud?" he asked as he walked by, patting me on the arm. From the deep resonance of his voice, he sounded like a big guy.

"All right," I replied and waited for his instructions. I was sitting with a group of seven people waiting to enter the haunted house at the Waikiki Shell. My friend Tasha and I had been talking about it for days. We hadn't been to a haunted house since we were kids, and on the drive over we were laughing and shivering like high schoolers.

The man started telling the group what to expect: there would be a lot of large stairs and a lot of low places where we would have to duck. He pointed the flashlight at me, the light glowing off of my cane. He said, "Especially you." I smiled and nodded. For one thing, I'm six foot eight, so I'm used to ducking through doorways and dodging ceiling fans. For another, I'm blind. Well, not completely blind, but close enough. I still have some sight at the periphery of my vision, but I carry a cane and borrow an occasional shoulder when walking through unfamiliar territory.

"We're together," I said, gesturing toward Tasha. "She'll help me through."

Monty Anderson

"This is a dangerous place," he said, and I couldn't help but wonder why anyone would create a public event that was dangerous—especially an event where there were sure to be children. The flashlight beam moved from me to Tasha. "You did see the sign out front, right?" 'Enter at your own risk.'" Tasha shook her head. He turned to the group. "Okay all you people hear me telling this guy that he's entering at his own risk. This is a dangerous place, and we're not responsible for anything that might happen." I cringed. Was this guy for real? I understood his concern, but why was he involving everybody else? Did he want witnesses?

"Don't worry," I said, "no lawsuits."

Finally I was out of the spotlight. He told the group that we needed a leader and asked for a volunteer. One of the group members said, "I want him," and gestured to me. I laughed and said "At your own risk pal." And the mood began to lighten.

He handed the flashlight to Tasha. "You be the leader." She handed the flashlight back. "I can't lead these people and help my friend at the same time."

"Then you two need to leave," he said. "Go back to the ticket counter and try to get your money back." I thought, leave? This guy was kicking us out? Tasha calmly explained to him that she could guide me but not the rest of the group.

"You know," he said, again pointing the flashlight at me, "I don't know why they even sold you a ticket. Why did you even come here in the first place? You're blind."

My arms were trembling, and my face was hot. I had two choices: I could either stand up and tell this guy off, or I could leave. I considered sticking around, but by that point the fun was gone. Trying to remain calm, I turned to my friend and said, "Let's go."

On the way out, Tasha made a point of telling the ticket takers and those at the ticket counters what had just happened. We were met with silence. There were no apologies. Were they shocked? Were they embarrassed? Or were they silently wondering what a blind guy was doing there?

Indeed, what was a blind guy doing at a haunted house? To me, the answer is obvious: to have fun. Of course I wouldn't experience the event on the same level as a sighted person; I would experience the event on different levels. I still have other senses, and when I'm with a friend, they usually describe the visual things.

People are often perplexed that I enjoy movies, the theater, and baseball games. There's more to a movie than just spectacle. There's more to a play or baseball game than just action. There's a universe of sounds: laughing, talking, the crack of the bat, and the excited cheers of those sitting around me. There's a garden of aromas: the warm buttery smell of popcorn; the sharp tang of mustard on hot dogs; and hot, crispy French fries. These may not be experiences most would consider fun—but I do.

Everyone has the right to participate in society. And if they want to participate, they should be encouraged, not shamed. There's no shame in wanting to enjoy life. Organizers of public events need to understand that society consists of many people with disabilities, and these people need to be considered when events are being organized. Arrangements should be made to allow them to participate. It's no fun to have someone tell you that you're not welcome because of a physical attribute—something which one has no control over.

A person with a disability is not an alien, not a creature from another planet, not subhuman or less worthy of dignity and respect than any other person. With a little assistance and ingenuity, a person with a physical impairment can overcome most obstacles. Just a few years ago a gentleman who is totally blind climbed to the top of Mt. Everest. As the immortal philosopher John Lennon once said, "There are no problems, only solutions."

The haunted house at the Waikiki Shell was a public event, and I'm a member of the public. I should not have been bullied and made to feel stupid for wanting to join in. Was he wrong for his concerns? Absolutely not. It was perfectly reasonable for an employee of a major event to check in with me and ask if I knew the risks. The problem was that even after I made it clear that I knew the risks and was willing to go on, he continued to bully me—even at one point questioning why the ticket sellers had let me in. He put the spotlight on me and kept it there, embarrassing me in front of a group of people.

I guarantee you that if someone talked to him the way he talked to me, he would have belted that person. For the most part, this is an issue of communication and respect, and not so much intent; however, I did certainly get the feeling that he wanted me gone.

Did I do the right thing? Should I have told him where to go? Should I have stormed up to the counter and demanded to see the manager? Would any of that have improved anything? Who knows? I did what I did. I'm not a hostile or confrontational person, but I feel it is important to speak out against discrimination wherever it may be lurking.

Letters From Dad

by Jennifer Bose

Jennifer Bose lives in Massachusetts and is a member of the Cambridge chapter of the National Federation of the Blind. She works as a researcher for the University of Massachusetts in Boston. She still enjoys canoeing in the summer and fall on vacation, and believes strongly that many more people, adults and children, can learn and benefit from Braille. Her personal story makes the point. Here is how she tells it:

Twenty years ago, before anyone I knew ever typed some sentences or paragraphs into a computer program and then clicked "Send," I was a young teenager, spending the summers of 1984 and 1985 at a girls' camp in Maine. These summers spent close

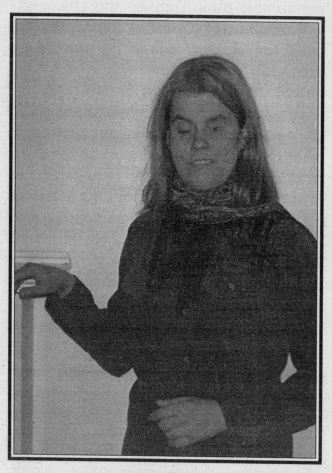

Jennifer Bose

to a beautiful lake offered exciting, memorable opportunities and challenges and adventures almost every day, except when the late June rainstorms squelched a canoe trip.

For daily excitement, though, we could always count on those moments after lunch when all of us—sixty or seventy teenage girls in blue shorts and T-shirts—would dash out of the dining room to comb the stacks of mail at the camp office. Somehow, with the staff's help, we would collect our letters and packages and troop back to our cabins in the woods to get a better look at everything during our after-lunch rest period.

While we devoured the contents of our mail—and our cabin mates' mail, too, if it contained candy or cookies—we would read letters from friends and family. The other girls retrieved their letters from stamped envelopes or read postcards, which was all, I admit, very interesting. I, however, would begin excitedly juggling an empty paper towel roll! On the outside of the paper towel roll was an address label. Taped inside was a rolled-up letter, in Braille, almost always from my dad. I would pull out the crisp pages, which had not been folded or crushed since they had been rolled up like a poster, and read my dad's latest newsy letter.

My dad, who is sighted, as everyone else is in my family, had learned Braille from the books, games, and alphabet cards my mom had collected during my earlier childhood so she and anyone else in the house could get a sense of Braille. In fact, everyone in the family had decided to use these tools to play with Braille or learn enough to write shorter messages or labels. But my dad, who wanted to write to me regularly at camp, learned the most Braille.

Even at 14 or 15, I knew that my dad treasured the letters I would dictate or type from camp and mail to him and the rest of the family. He had gone to summer camp for many of his early years and had also worked as a camp counselor, so he could appreciate the fun I was having and the new ways I was growing while memorizing sailors' knots, participating in swim races, trying out for the crew team, and learning to get along well with other cabin mates. By learning Braille, he communicated any of his advice or reactions directly to me.

Over the years, my dad got even better at Braille than before. He, like everyone in the family, loved letters and words, whether in novels, newspapers, or word games. For my dad, the crossword puzzle fanatic, learning Braille was like cracking an exciting code that would make it easier for him to be understood by me in writing.

When I visited home during my college years, he would always ask me how to write a particular punctuation mark or letter, scrawling the dot combination in a little note to himself anywhere he could. These days, he still gets out the Perkins Brailler and carefully "bangs out" a letter whenever he wants to make sure I have something in writing from him. For example, when it comes to finances, he always has great advice about financial planning and how to keep records. His knowledge of Braille makes it easy for him to write about anything confidential, whether financial or personal, that he would like me to be able to read directly, without the need to scan anything or show the letter to a reader.

Nowadays, with the benefit of technology, my dad would never need to scribble down a dot combination or haul out the bulky Perkins Brailler to bang out more pages of Braille. Certainly, he could make his life easier by using Braille translation software and a Braille printer to produce those pages.

The availability of this technology notwithstanding, his realization of the importance and benefits of Braille was what drove him to learn it himself and be able to recognize those dot patterns. I will always appreciate his excited attitude toward learning a writing system many people dismiss as too frustrating. For my dad, the letter-writer, crossword sleuth and finance guy, the payoffs—including my ability to read one of his letters from home while at summer camp—were worth the investment!

IF I COULD CHOOSE

by Robert M. Eschbach

Robert Eschbach is a retired Methodist minister. He has served as president of the National Federation of the Blind of Ohio and as a member of our National Board. With the skill of the preacher that he is, Rev. Eschbach crafts an important message for all of us to ponder in his story, "If I Could Choose." Here is what he has to say:

I love to walk. I don't do it for the exercise or for the health benefits, but I have always enjoyed the ability just to ramble where I wanted to go under my own steam. Even as a child growing up in the mountains of the Philippines, I walked everywhere and thoroughly enjoyed investigating trails, fishing for tadpoles in a stream, hiking through beautiful pine forests, and generally discovering the delights of what nature had to offer.

After I became blind, I continued walking everywhere. In those days all that blind people had to help us were waisthigh wooden canes with crooks for handles. These were painted white with big red tips. When I look back on it, I am amazed at all we did with those little canes. At least using them meant that we didn't have to wait around for someone to take us places. But walking was the main thing.

Unfortunately I had weak ankles. In time I was forced to wear shoes that would allow me to continue doing what I liked to do. As the years went by, these ankles of mine argued with me more and more, but I walked anyway. Of course the time came when I had to slow down, yield to the need to ride in a car instead, getting around the way most people did. Eventually arthritis took over, and there were times when I

Robert Eschbach

actually had to hobble a few steps before my ankles would let me begin moving with relative ease.

My wife and I enjoy traveling with our motor home. Several years ago we went with an RV caravan into Eastern Canada. It was a delightful venture, and we made many friends as we marveled at the remarkable ways nature works. We watched and listened to the tidal bore, watching ducks trying to swim downstream when one of these tides was coming in and seeing them go backwards. We tasted all kinds of foods not generally available back home, and we investigated wilderness areas that still seemed to be untouched by humankind.

As we visited Peggy's Cove, I really struggled to get to the places we wanted to explore. We had to climb over and around huge boulders and use lots of steps to get to lookout points. My wife had to assist me because my ankles were protesting.

Several days after this adventure we had to leave the caravan and return home for a wedding. The night before we left, we gave each person in our new circle of friends a Kernel Book published by the National Federation of the Blind, and I read one of the articles aloud, demonstrating that blind people can read Braille as efficiently as sighted people read print.

The article, written by Barbara Pierce, was titled "Fighting Every Step of the Way." In the article Barbara describes the frustrations of dealing with people who believe absolutely that blind adults cannot safely negotiate independently or, for that matter, be counted upon to get anywhere safely.

As I read, I realized that the folks around me had probably assumed that all the difficulties I had been experiencing in walking were caused by my blindness. I asked point-blank, "Do you folks think that I have trouble getting around because I'm blind?" The response was a universal and emphatic yes. So I explained that blindness had nothing to do with it; arthritis was the culprit. Using Barbara's article as the backdrop, I described many of the things blind people can do.

Not long ago I was walking past the TV while my wife Pat was watching the Oprah Winfrey show. Oprah was asking members of the audience the question, "If you could change anything in your life right now, what would it be?"

I muttered "ankles." Then I thought, "What would have happened if I had been asked that question on her show?" I can guarantee that she would have been astounded that my answer was not "blindness." I smiled as I reflected on such a hypothetical exchange. I believe my response would have rendered her speechless—an unusual state for her.

But the reality is that I have been blind for much of my life, and it has never stopped me from doing what I wanted to do, but arthritis certainly has.

IT'S NO BIG DEAL!

by Mark Feliz

Mark Feliz is president of the East Valley Chapter of the National Federation of the Blind of Arizona. He is a father, a teacher, and a skilled mechanic. He views the fact that he also happens to be blind as incidental to the person he is and the life he leads. As he puts it, it's no big deal! Here is how he tells his story:

Ah yes, when the ignition key is turned, and the engine kicks over to a smooth gentle hummmm—no horrid grinding, no springs or doodads flying everywhere, and most importantly, NO SPARE PARTS, you know that is success.

Fixing engine problems, lawn mowers, large and small appliances, and carpentry work were (and for the most part are) commonplace with me.

I became blind by the age of eighteen months from Retino Blastoma, which is cancer of the retinas. After both eyes were removed, and I was fitted with prosthetic eyes, my parents bundled me up and took me home. Although they knew nothing of the National Federation of the Blind, by some miracle they raised me under most of the same philosophy that the National Federation of the Blind teaches.

My parents had an energetic two-year-old on their hands who happened to be blind. They relied on intuition in guiding them to make difficult decisions. Since we lived in a very small town, all the children had the run of the town as their play yard—and so did I. I ran through the town with my older brother. He and I were constantly being reprimanded for getting into mischief. If he rode his tricycle, I was close behind him. If he jumped dirt hills on his bicycle, I was close behind. If he roller-skated through the town, again I was close behind.

Of course, not being a cane user at that time I did have many run-ins with large, sharp, or hazardous objects that just refused to move out of my way. So basically, my parents felt I was "normal" in every respect except I couldn't see. Of course, their attitude or philosophy was not perfect. As mentioned above, I did not use a cane until I began grade school at Arizona State School for the Deaf and Blind. However, considering they had no real guidance, it is pretty amazing how much their attitudes and philosophy paralleled that of the National Federation of the Blind.

There was never any question of, "Will I be unable to do something because I am blind?" If there was a task to be done, such as chores around the house, building a fort in the backyard, helping dad repair the car, or taking my turn in yard work, alternative techniques to accomplish these tasks were automatically developed. I am very fortunate to have grown up in this environment. Those attitudes, I believe, are what have allowed me to become who I am now. And meeting and recognizing the National Federation of the Blind nineteen years ago, further validated that who I am and what I do are "not" anything spectacular or super heroic.

I am Mark Feliz with a master of education degree. I have a wife and three children and have been teaching at the public school level for fourteen years. There are many things about me I could continue to mention; most I am proud of, a few I am not. And among those things that can be mentioned is the fact that I happen to be blind.

Now, the question of the year is, "How do we as blind people change the attitudes of the general population also to believe that blind people are just like they are?" I believe we can do this through the process of exposure. When my brother is having trouble with his truck he may stop by, and we look at it together. He doesn't give this a second thought.

This same brother however, would not take his truck to our younger brother simply because this brother knows very little of auto repair. On occasion there may be a friend of my brother's present when we are repairing his truck or some such task. And, of course, his friend is amazed that I am able to participate in the task at hand. I am the super heroic human being, possessing unique and privileged powers.

I am sure we've all experienced these circumstances. At this point it is my responsibility to change the attitudes and impressions of this friend. They must be changed to the point where this same friend can stand alongside of me without a second thought. He should not be mystified by every little thing I do. This is my responsibility as a member of the National Federation of the Blind.

A Silent Compliment

by Michael Freeman

Michael Freeman is president of the National Federation of the Blind of Washington state and has built a successful career in the high-tech industry. Here he describes a small incident which took place recently while dining with a friend at a local restaurant—an incident which as he reflected on it—pleased him very much. Here is what he has to say:

Like most blind people, I am accustomed to restaurant personnel who are uncomfortable interacting with me. This discomfort is partly due to the fact that they cannot spontaneously make eye contact with me without speaking, and partly due to the fact that they have probably interacted with few, if any, blind persons. (We are a

Michael Freeman

very small minority in society.) If I am with a sighted companion, it is common to hear my companion being asked, "What would he like to drink?" or "Would he like cream and sugar in his coffee?"

I usually deal with this by turning to the waiter or waitress and simply smiling and answering the question. Although this doesn't always work—I was once asked by a waitress in a Mexican restaurant if I knew what I was eating—it usually gets the point across that I am competent and that interacting with me is easy. Last weekend, however, I encountered a novel situation at a local steak-and-seafood restaurant. While some blind persons might have taken it to be a sign of ignorance or even neglect on the part of the waitress, I considered it a compliment, albeit one without words.

I had taken a partially sighted companion to dinner. We had not been to this particular restaurant in several months; however, the manager remembered me. The waitress had not met me before. She handed both my companion and me print menus, but upon being informed that neither my companion nor I could read them, had no trouble shifting mental gears and reading the menus as necessary.

All through dinner the waitress used common sense, simply asking me if I wished refills of coffee or if my companion and I wanted dessert (we did). We interacted so easily with the waitress that I think blindness no longer was much of an issue for her. This was as it should have been. With proper training and opportunity, blindness can be reduced to being a physical nuisance—a nuisance which does not interfere with the enjoyment of life, gastronomically or otherwise.

As my companion and I lingered over our after-dessert coffee, I began to wonder what had become of the bill. I did not think the waitress had presented it to my companion; she would have protested and just handed the bill to me. Nor had my companion told me that the bill was being placed in front of me. She is losing her vision but can still see a fair amount under certain conditions. I did not think to search for the bill, as waiters and waitresses at this restaurant usually make a bit of a to-do when they bring the bill. So my companion and I sat drinking our coffee and engaging in pleasant conversation.

Finally, we decided that it was time to leave and let other patrons have our places. I flagged down the waitress and asked her for the bill. I was told in some astonishment that the bill was beside me on the table; bills at this restaurant come in an elegant little leather notebook that has a place to put one's credit card which the waiter or waitress takes to be processed.

I reached out and, sure enough, there was the little notebook. I sheepishly put my credit card in the proper place, and the book was spirited away to process the bill. My companion said that she hadn't even seen the bill book because it was black and didn't show up well to her against the background of the table. We both laughed, and I gave the waitress a healthy tip when she returned with my credit card and credit card slip.

As we waited for a taxi (busses don't run late in the evening on weekends), I pondered what had just occurred. Some blind people, I mused, might have become irritated, thinking that the waitress should have told me that she had presented the bill. It seemed to me, however, that such a reaction would be misplaced.

Although it might have been helpful for the waitress to tell me the bill was there, I certainly could have searched for it myself. And I further thought that the waitress had paid me the supreme, if tacit, compliment of presuming that I would find the bill and deal with it myself. She was right; once I came to my senses and knew the bill was there, I handled things in the usual way and only needed her to show me where to affix my signature on the credit card slip.

We are all used to being complimented out loud. Silence can also be a compliment.

PUTTING UP THE CHRISTMAS TREE

by Nathanael Wales

For all of us—blind and sighted alike— there are building blocks of personal experience from which we construct the joyful traditions in our lives. In "Putting Up the Christmas Tree," Nathanael Wales shares one such building block important in his life. Nathanael first came to the National Federation of the Blind as a high school student. Now he is a successful engineer living in California. He contributes his time and many talents to furthering the work of the National Federation of the Blind. Here is what he has to say:

The evening five days before Christmas was what had turned out to be a quiet evening with my friend, a blind student at the

University of California at Berkeley, and her roommate at their apartment a few miles off campus. We were preparing for the Christmas holiday, exchanging gifts, drinking hot chocolate, and thinking of going out to a wonderful Italian restaurant a few blocks from the campus. It occurred to us, though, that the decor of her apartment was not complete for Christmas: the apartment needed a Christmas tree. So before we left for dinner, we decided to fix that.

My friend has an artificial Christmas tree. Of course, a real tree may be more festive, but the plastic one was more efficient for apartment living. We took our canes and went outside to her storage closet, retrieved the tree which was packed in a long and narrow box, and pulled out another larger box filled with several strings of Christmas lights and three different garlands.

For many years when I was growing up, my family also had an artificial Christmas

Nathanael Wales

tree instead of a real one. My father had always set it up and strung the lights. Only afterwards would my sister and I hang the various ornaments my family had. This would be my first time setting up a Christmas tree. I was a bit unsure as to how it should be done, and being a bit of a perfectionist I wanted it to look good visually. I decided to approach the problem as a puzzle.

As an engineer, that seemed very logical and practical. And it would be sort of an adventure both for my friend who is blind and for me, too. Although we have met many blind people who have done some very interesting mechanical things—from building all manner of works of carpentry to overhauling an automobile engine— neither of us had yet met another blind person who had assembled and decorated an artificial Christmas tree before.

So we set to work. We went back into my friend's living room and first unpacked the long, narrow box containing the artificial tree. My friend laid out the cloth apron for the tree on the floor. This apron was, for the plastic tree, more aesthetic than necessary.

Next, I assembled the plastic trunk and supports for the tree. The trunk was designed in three segments: the bottom segment into which the tripod supports attached and into which the bottom branches attached, the middle segment into which yet more branches attached, and the top segment into which the top branches attached and which had at the very top four small, symmetrical branches. I found the assembly of the trunk and supports relatively easy; the segments simply slid together.

Next, I had to put together the three dimensional puzzle of which branches went where. There were three general types of branches: very short ones with needles all over which could be fluffed out, medium ones with needles primarily at the ends, and long ones with needles all over. It seemed logical that the shortest ones should attach at the top of the trunk. After that, it seemed logical that the medium and medium-to-long branches with needles only at the ends should be attached generally in the middle of the trunk. As with putting together any puzzle, it was necessary a few times to switch branches from one level to another if we felt some perceptible inconsistency in the tapered result we wanted.

Finally, I attached the long branches with needles all over to the lowermost segment, still keeping in mind the tapered end product we wanted. Again, the ends of each branch easily slid into small grooves protruding slightly from the trunk. As I attached each branch, my friend fluffed out the artificial needles with her hand to give the tree fullness.

With the plastic tree assembled, we then strung the Christmas lights. We began by plugging into the wall the main junction box from which the first set of strings of lights originated. My friend, her roommate, and I stood around the tree and passed the end of each string around. Each of us attached it to opportune branches by making a sort of loop out of the double cords connecting each bulb. We began with the lowest branches and worked up to the top as we passed the strings around among us.

After two different sets of lights, the tree was perfectly well lit; the multitude of small, glowing bulbs made the plastic tree slightly warmer. The final string of lights contained a star with a bulb in it; we bent the top four branches slightly up to delicately balance the star on the top of the tree. I felt a bit of pride in the placement of that star because, in a small way, it marked what was a first accomplishment for me.

Finally, we strung the three garlands around the tree. Again, my friend, her roommate, and I stood around the tree and passed each garland around. We worked from the bottom of the tree to the top, resting the garland over the branches as we worked. With the third garland around, the Christmas tree was put up and well decorated.

With the Christmas tree put up and well decorated, my friend's living room was ready for the Christmas holiday. The brightness and warmth of the tree in her apartment was a wonderful reflection of the warmth of the hot chocolate in our bodies, the joy of our time together, and the warmth of the season in our souls.

And with the Christmas tree put up and well decorated, I had the joy of participating in Christmas in a way in which I never quite had before as a blind person. Perhaps next year I will get a Christmas tree for my own apartment. I may even get a real one. And perhaps I will share this story as a small gift to other blind people so that they can know they can put up the Christmas tree, too.

I Was a Teenage Easter Bunny

by Tami Dodd Jones

Today Tami Dodd Jones is a mother and has been a successful teacher of blind children for many years. She is also an active leader in the National Federation of the Blind. Here she reminisces about her first real paying job— a rather unusual one as a teenage Easter bunny. Here is how she tells her story:

My first real part-time paying job began during my sophomore year of college. Prior to that, I had resisted the temptation to earn a little extra money, because I was attending school on a scholarship, which required me to maintain good grades in all my classes. I had been afraid to commit to a job that would reduce my study time every week on a continuing basis. Then, my mom of all people clued me in about a part-time seasonal job she felt was right up my alley.

Mom often took on extra work, and the previous December, she had acted as a photographer's assistant for one of our local malls. So, in early March, she learned they were looking for a few temporary employees to help with the Easter photography project. In short, the mall was looking for people who could work as Easter bunnies.

Now this job wasn't as easy as it sounds. You had to work lots of evening and weekend hours, wear a thick floppy costume that would have kept you warm during a January blizzard, and walk around wearing a thirty-pound papier-mâché bunny head with no eyeholes. The only light that entered the head came from several small holes on either side of the bunny's cute buckteeth.

Although the mall had had many applicants, most people wouldn't work

Tami Dodd Jones

under those conditions for what they were willing to pay, or were too clumsy, or were just plain freaked out by not being able to see the people and objects around them clearly. Of course, this didn't bother me; I have had very limited vision most of my life and had completed a course in orientation and mobility just a few years before, in which I used sleep shades (a type of blindfold) and a long white cane to travel independently all over the city. Even without a cane, I was confident I could do a really good job.

The afternoon before my first day of work, I caught a city bus out to the mall. I wanted to figure out the best route to get to my job. I found the mall office, and the assistant manager showed me the dressing room and the time clock.

She gave me my timecard, and I attached a small piece of plastic Dymo tape with my initials Brailled on it to the top edge, the part that wouldn't actually go into the machine. She showed me the route I must take from the dressing room to the platform with the big white wicker chair, where I would sit with children on my lap as the photographer took pictures. I was really excited!

The next day I took the bus to the mall a little early, so I walked around about thirty minutes before clocking in. My card was right where I had left it, so this didn't take much time. I found the dressing room, and exchanged my slacks and long-sleeved shirt for shorts and a T-shirt. I was really glad I did, because when I climbed into my costume, I immediately started to sweat. Then I had to wait for the bunny head.

Although every employee had her own costume, we all shared one head, which was sprayed with disinfectant after every person's shift was over. The head was large, heavy and hand-made, so duplicating it would have been expensive, and storage between Easter seasons could have been a problem.

My co-worker's shift was finally over, and it was my turn. I balanced the head on my shoulders, and I discovered that I had to move my head very slowly and carefully to keep the head from overbalancing or shifting. If I leaned over too far, the head, which was over three feet tall from chin to ear tips, would be in danger of falling off. I had a few close calls at first, but I quickly got the knack.

The photographer walked me to the platform the first day, but later, after he learned I was fine on my own, he let me find my own way. The area behind the stage was roped off, so there were no people to run into. I would casually trail the wall to the platform, and then follow the platform around to the steps. It was easy after that.

There were five steps up, and the chair was just three steps beyond the top stair. All I had to do was sit in the chair and wait for the photographer's assistant to lead a child up to me. Then, I would invite him or her up onto my lap, or would place the child there myself using my mitten-like bunny hands. Sometimes I would talk, and sometimes I wouldn't, depending on the circumstances. Sometimes I would sing the Peter Cottontail song or recite a nursery rhyme—whatever it took to get the child to sit still and smile. After the picture had been taken, the assistant would come back and lead the child back down the stairs, while I waved good-bye. Then the whole process would start again.

This went on non-stop for about an hour and a half, after which I got a fifteen-minute break to go back to the dressing room. There I could take off my head, get a drink or use the bathroom. Then it would be time to go back out to meet the public once again.

Depending on how long I was working that day, I might get a half-hour meal break. I usually spent this time in the dressing room, eating a sack lunch. Although I would always climb out of my costume to cool down, I didn't want to have to change into my street clothes until my shift was over.

During March, I usually worked from 15-25 hours per week, four to six hours per shift. During spring break, I worked even more, picking up extra hours as employees quit or were let go for one reason or another. One bunny became a photographer's assistant, so the rest of us divided up her shifts. I gradually built up quite a little nest egg.

This pattern continued right through the day before Easter with a very few exceptions. Once the mall agreed to bring their Easter bunny to a local nursery school. So, I suited up and was led to the nearest exit, where a van was waiting. I climbed in, but had to sit on the floor; the bunny ears were too tall for me to sit on the seat.

When we arrived at the school, I climbed out, and the kids were right there, ready to greet me. I got lots of hugs and pats and handshakes. I handed out candy and eggs and coloring books advertising the mall. They all told me their names, and I tried hard to match the names with the voices. This is something I do regularly, so I didn't make too many mistakes. The kids were impressed, and so was my boss.

After about forty minutes, it was time to leave. I made my way back to the van, led by two children holding my hands. They didn't know I couldn't see; they just wanted to be with me as long as possible. I felt really good! Back at the mall, it was business as usual, but the memory of how happy those kids were to see me, helped make the hours fly.

Other incidents stick in my mind. One Saturday, some of the guys from my co-ed dorm came to the mall and were fooling around. Four of them decided to get their pictures taken with the Easter bunny. Now they didn't really know me—at least well enough to know where I worked—but I recognized their voices. One guy perched on each of my knees, and the other two knelt on either side of me. While the photographer was setting up his shot, the guy on my right knee turned to me and asked, "Are you a girl rabbit or a boy rabbit?" I just laughed and left him guessing.

Another time a close friend visited me at the mall, and got his picture taken sitting on my lap, complete with long white cane. A few years later, he died from diabetic complications, so that particular picture means a lot to me.

I worked for the mall three Easter seasons in a row, until they contracted the work out to some big outfit that did the same thing in malls throughout the Midwest. By then, I was about to graduate, and was interested in work of a more permanent sort. However, I will never forget my first real paid work experience, and I still get a kick out of telling people how I was a teenage Easter bunny.

OTHER KERNEL BOOKS

To Touch the Untouchable Dream

Remember to Feed the Kittens

Reflecting the Flame

Oh, Wow!

I Can Feel Blue on Monday

*Reaching for the Top in the
Land Down Under*

Safari

Summit

Not Much of a Muchness

The Car, the Sled, and the Butch Wax

To Reach for the Stars

The Lessons of the Earth

You can help us spread the word...

...about our *Braille Readers Are Leaders* contest for blind schoolchildren, a project which encourages blind children to achieve literacy through Braille.

...about our scholarships for deserving blind college students.

...about NFB-NEWSLINE®, a free service that allows blind persons to read the newspaper over the telephone.

...about where to turn for accurate information about blindness and the abilities of the blind.

Most importantly, you can help us by sharing what you've learned about blindness in these pages with your family and friends. If you know anyone who needs assistance with the problems of blindness, please write:

Marc Maurer, President
National Federation of the Blind
1800 Johnson Street, Suite 300
Baltimore, Maryland 21230-4998

Other Ways You Can Help the National Federation of the Blind

Write to us for tax-saving information on bequests and planned giving programs.

OR

Include the following language in your will:

"I give, devise, and bequeath unto National Federation of the Blind, 1800 Johnson Street, Suite 300, Baltimore, Maryland 21230, a District of Columbia nonprofit corporation, the sum of $_____ (or "____ percent of my net estate" or "The following stocks and bonds:_____") to be used for its worthy purposes on behalf of blind persons."

Your Contributions Are Tax-deductible